I can count
Sé contar

Bobbie Kalman

 Crabtree Publishing Company

www.crabtreebooks.com

Created by Bobbie Kalman

Author and Editor-in-Chief
Bobbie Kalman

Educational consultants
Elaine Hurst
Joan King
Reagan Miller

Editors
Joan King
Reagan Miller
Kathy Middleton

Proofreader
Crystal Sikkens

Design
Bobbie Kalman
Katherine Berti

Photo research
Bobbie Kalman

Production coordinator
Katherine Berti

Prepress technician
Katherine Berti

Photographs by Shutterstock

Library and Archives Canada Cataloguing in Publication

Available at Library and Archives Canada

Library of Congress Cataloging-in-Publication Data

Available at Library of Congress

Crabtree Publishing Company

www.crabtreebooks.com   1-800-387-7650

Printed in China/082010/AP20100512

Published in Canada
Crabtree Publishing
616 Welland Ave.
St. Catharines, Ontario
L2M 5V6

Published in the United States
Crabtree Publishing
PMB 59051
350 Fifth Avenue, 59th Floor
New York, New York 10118

Published in the United Kingdom
Crabtree Publishing
Maritime House
Basin Road North, Hove
BN41 1WR

Published in Australia
Crabtree Publishing
386 Mt. Alexander Rd.
Ascot Vale (Melbourne)
VIC 3032

Words to know
Palabras que debo saber

ant
hormiga

bird
pájaro

butterfly
mariposa

cat
gato

caterpillar
oruga

dog
perro

fish
pez

horse
caballo

rabbit
conejo

snake
serpiente

I can count zero dogs.

Sé contar cero perros.

4

1

I can count one dog.

Sé contar un perro.

I can count two caterpillars.

Sé contar dos orugas.

3

I can count three horses.

Sé contar tres caballos.

4

I can count four cats.

Sé contar cuatro gatos.

5

I can count five ants.

Sé contar cinco hormigas.

6

I can count six rabbits.

Sé contar seis conejos.

I can count seven birds.

Sé contar siete pájaros.

I can count eight butterflies.

Sé contar ocho mariposas.

I can count nine fish.

Sé contar nueve peces.

10

I can count ten snakes.

Sé contar diez serpientes.

Activity

Can you count zero fish?

Can you count one fish?

Can you count two fish?

Can you count three fish?

Can you count six fish?

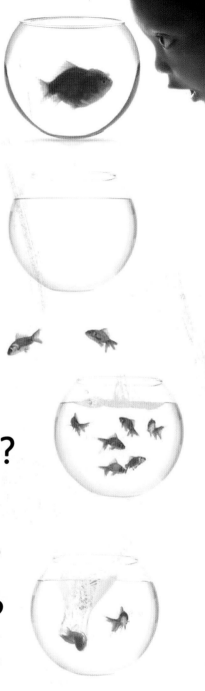

Actividad

¿Puedes contar cero peces?

¿Puedes contar un pez?

¿Puedes contar dos peces?

¿Puedes contar tres peces?

¿Puedes contar seis peces?

15

Notes for adults

Counting living things

I can count introduces children to numbers and counting, as well as reading. Counting living things is an excellent way to teach children numbers. When you go for a walk, ask the children to count the people, squirrels, or dogs they see. Some things move, so the numbers may not be the same on the way back. They may be left with zero dogs or squirrels! Counting things that move is also a good introduction to adding and subtracting. Use the fishbowl on page 15 as an introduction. How have the number of fish in each bowl changed? How many fish will be in each bowl when the jumping fish are added? How many were there before the fish jumped out of the bowls?

"I can count" books

A fun activity for children is to make their own "I can count" books. For each number, ask them to include the number word, number symbol, and a pictorial representation of the number. Children can use stickers, cut out pictures from magazines, or draw colorful shapes to represent each number. Once a child has mastered numbers zero through ten, more pages with higher numbers can be added to the book.

Notas para los adultos

Contar cosas vivientes

Sé contar invita a los niños a conocer los números y a contar, así como a leer. Contar cosas vivientes es una manera excelente de enseñarles los números a los niños. Cada vez que salgan a caminar pídales que cuenten las personas, las ardillas o los perros que vean. Algunas cosas se mueven, por lo tanto puede ser que la cantidad no sea la misma al regreso. ¡Tal vez no haya ningún perro o ardilla que contar! Contar cosas que se mueven es una buena introducción a la suma y a la resta. Use la pecera de la página 15 como introducción. ¿En qué cambió el número de peces de cada pecera? ¿Cuántos peces habrá en cada pecera después de que se agreguen los peces saltarines? ¿Cuántos peces había en las peceras antes de que saltaran fuera de ellas?

Libros "Sé contar"

Una actividad divertida para los niños es que hagan sus propios libros "Sé contar." Para cada número pídales que incluyan el número en palabras, su símbolo numérico y una representación gráfica del número. Los niños pueden usar calcomanías, pueden recortar figuras de revistas o pueden dibujar figuras coloridas para representar cada número. Una vez que los niños dominen los números del cero al diez, se le podrán agregar más páginas al libro con números mayores.